1 1

HARRY
Kane

Ben Hubbard

raintree

a Capstone company — publishers for children

Raintree is an imprint of Capstone Global Library Limited, a company incorporated in England and Wales having its registered office at 264 Banbury Road, Oxford, OX2 7DY – Registered company number: 6695582

www.raintree.co.uk
myorders@raintree.co.uk

Editor: Helen Cox Cannons
Designer: Justin Hoffmann at Pixelfox
Media researcher: Morgan Walters
Production specialist: Kathy McColley

ISBN 978 1 4747 7713 1 (hardback)
ISBN 978 1 4747 7715 5 (paperback)

British Library Cataloguing in Publication Data
A full catalogue record for this book is available from the British Library.

Acknowledgements
We would like to thank the following for permission to reproduce photographs: Alamy: dpa picture alliance, 5; Newscom: Andrew Couldridge/ZUMA Press, spread 18-19, FAM14648/Famous/Avalon, 7, Peter Cziborra/ZUMA Press, 17; Shutterstock: chrisdorney, 9, Cosminlftode, Cover, Dokshin Vlad, 26, Kurt Pacaud, 13, Marco Iacobucci EPP, 23, spread 24-25, 31, Photo Works, 10, Ververidis Vasilis, 21, Willy Barton, spread 14-15.

Every effort has been made to contact copyright holders of material reproduced in this book. Any omissions will be rectified in subsequent printings if notice is given to the publisher.

CONTENTS

CHAPTER 1

FOOTBALL SUPERSTAR!

It's England's opening match of the 2018 World Cup. They are playing Tunisia. The match has reached **injury time**. The score is 1–1. Millions of eyes are on Harry Kane. Harry is England's main **striker** and captain. Can he take the team to victory?

In the 91st minute, England have a corner. The ball crosses to Harry at the post. He heads it into the back of the net. Goooaaaaallll!!!!!!!! England have won the match!

Harry's header made him an England hero.

5

Today, Harry Kane is one of the world's best footballers. He has scored over 110 goals for his club Tottenham Hotspur. He has won many awards. He is paid millions every year to play football.

He is one of England's most famous faces. But getting to the top has not been easy. There have been many disappointments along the way.

When Harry was 12 years old, he met his hero David Beckham (left). Harry has worked hard to reach the top, like Beckham did.

CHAPTER 2

KICKING ABOUT

Harry Kane was born on 28 July 1993. He grew up in North London. From the beginning, football was in Harry's blood. Harry's grandfather had been a footballer. His family were Tottenham Hotspur fans. Harry's dream was to become a striker for Tottenham.

SETBACKS

"I had setbacks but I still always had that belief that I was going to play for Tottenham Hotspur."
Harry Kane

Harry grew up a few miles from Tottenham Hotspur's stadium, White Hart Lane.

Jermain Defoe scored 91 goals for Tottenham between 2004 and 2014.

10

Harry often kicked a football about with his friends after school. They would play on the street outside his home. They stopped to let cars pass. But one day an expensive car pulled up beside them. The driver was Jermain Defoe!

Defoe was a famous Tottenham footballer. He asked if he could join the game. Harry couldn't believe he was playing against one of his heroes!

CHAPTER 3

THE CLUB PLAYER

When he was aged eight, Harry played for the **youth club** Ridgeway Rovers. David Beckham used to play for Ridgeway too. One day, **scouts** came to watch Harry play. They offered him a place at Arsenal Football Club's youth **academy**.

Arsenal are Tottenham's biggest rivals, so Harry was not sure. But he joined Arsenal anyway. However, this only lasted for one year. Arsenal then said they no longer wanted Harry. It was a huge disappointment.

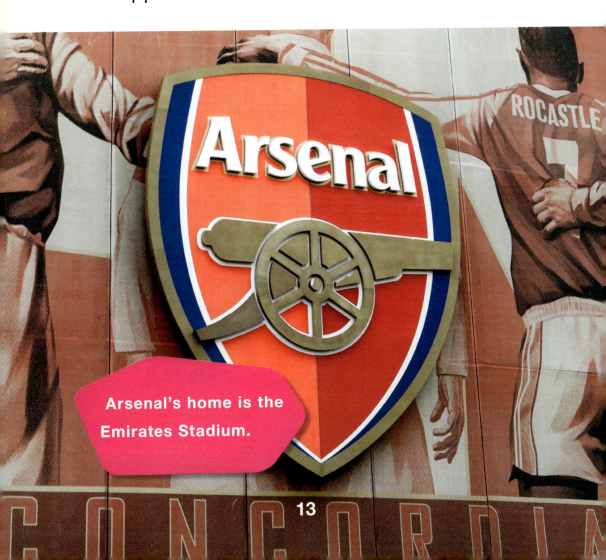

Arsenal's home is the Emirates Stadium.

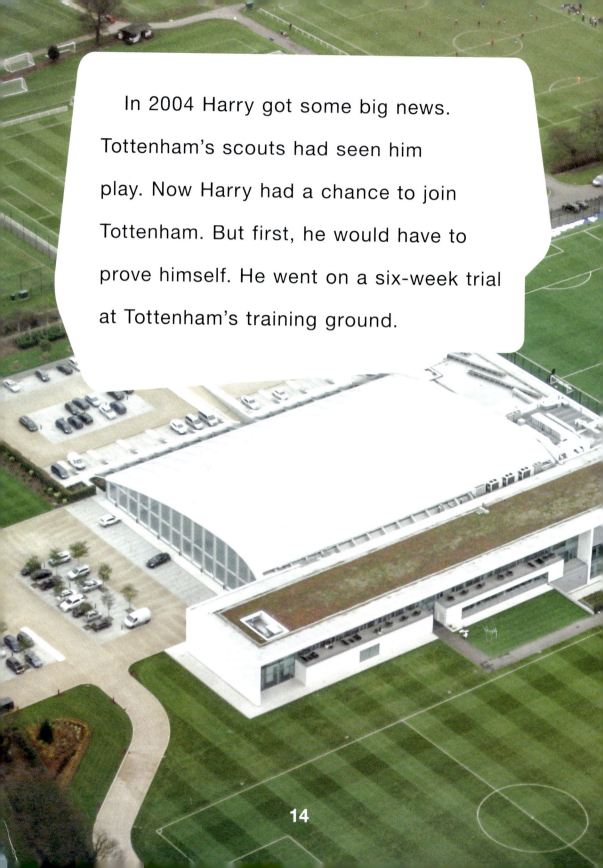

In 2004 Harry got some big news. Tottenham's scouts had seen him play. Now Harry had a chance to join Tottenham. But first, he would have to prove himself. He went on a six-week trial at Tottenham's training ground.

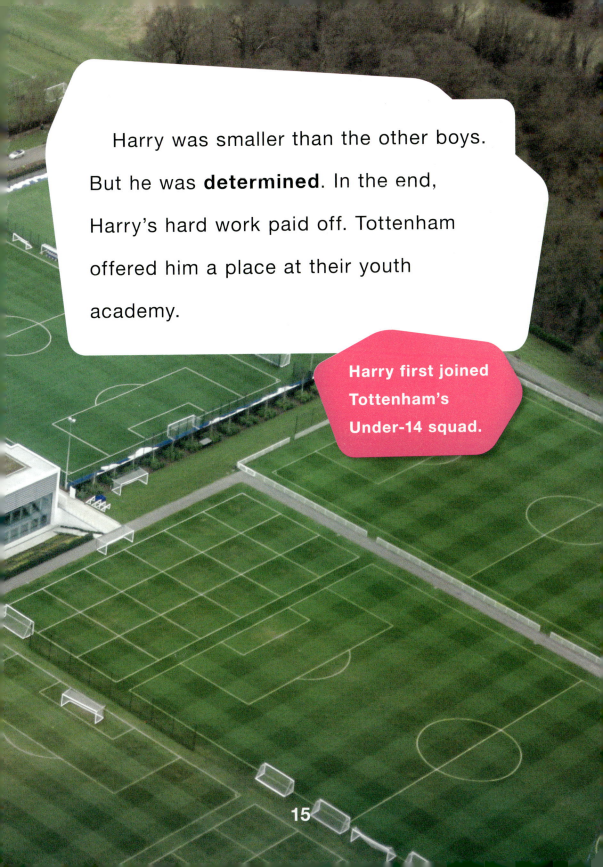

Harry was smaller than the other boys. But he was **determined**. In the end, Harry's hard work paid off. Tottenham offered him a place at their youth academy.

Harry first joined Tottenham's Under-14 squad.

CHAPTER 4

TOTTENHAM HOTSPUR

Harry did well at Tottenham. He moved through the club's youth academy. When he was age 16, Harry scored 18 goals for Tottenham. In 2010 he signed his first senior contract. But then there was some difficult news. Tottenham were sending Harry out on **loan**. He was then sent out on loan a further three times.

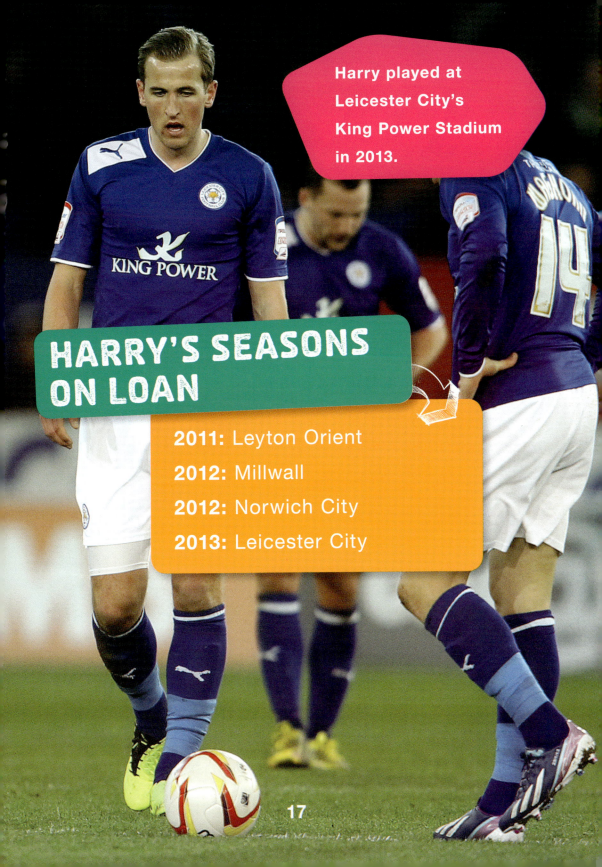

Harry played at Leicester City's King Power Stadium in 2013.

HARRY'S SEASONS ON LOAN

2011: Leyton Orient

2012: Millwall

2012: Norwich City

2013: Leicester City

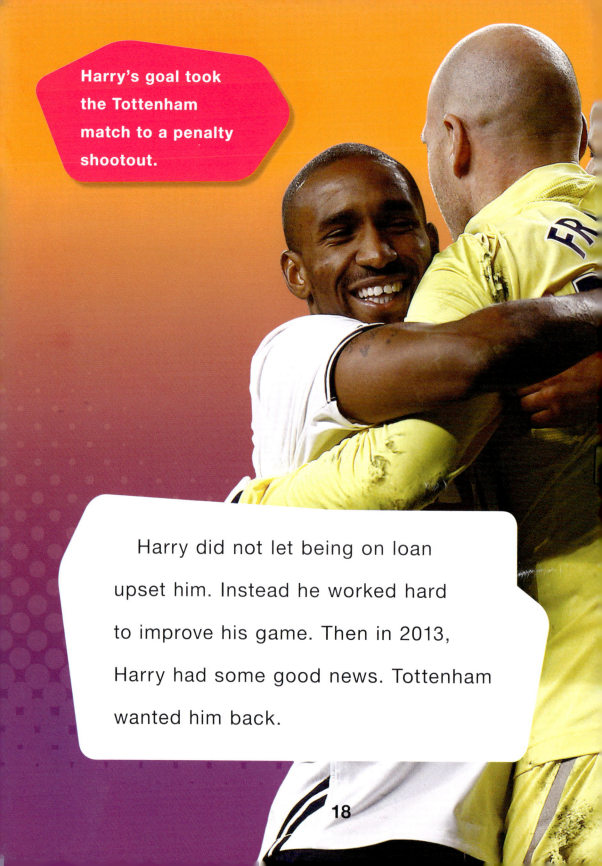

Harry's goal took the Tottenham match to a penalty shootout.

Harry did not let being on loan upset him. Instead he worked hard to improve his game. Then in 2013, Harry had some good news. Tottenham wanted him back.

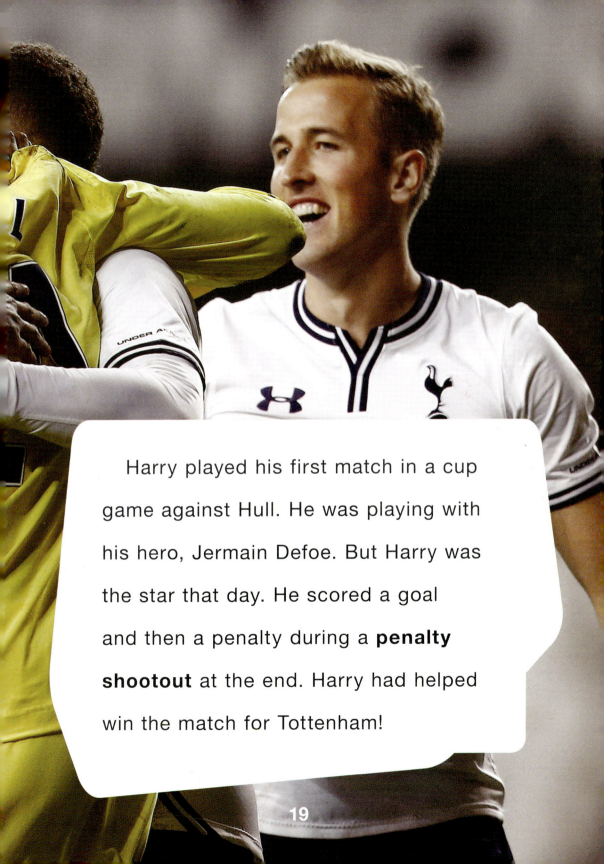

Harry played his first match in a cup game against Hull. He was playing with his hero, Jermain Defoe. But Harry was the star that day. He scored a goal and then a penalty during a **penalty shootout** at the end. Harry had helped win the match for Tottenham!

By 2015, Harry was on fire. He had become a goal-scoring machine for Tottenham. He was named Premier League Player of the Month twice. He became the Premier League's top scorer for two seasons in a row. Harry then signed a new contract until 2020. He was becoming a Tottenham legend.

HARRY'S SHIRT NUMBER

Jermain Defoe gave Harry his number 18 shirt when he left Tottenham. Later, Harry was given the famous number 10 shirt. This was a great honour.

21

CHAPTER 5

HARRY PLAYS FOR ENGLAND

In 2015, Harry got the phone call every English footballer dreams of. He would be playing in the national England squad. Harry's first England match was against Lithuania. He scored 80 seconds after coming on.

In 2018, Harry became only the third England player to score a **hat trick** during a World Cup match.

Later that year, Harry scored five goals against San Marino. In 2017, he was named England captain. He was becoming like his hero, David Beckham.

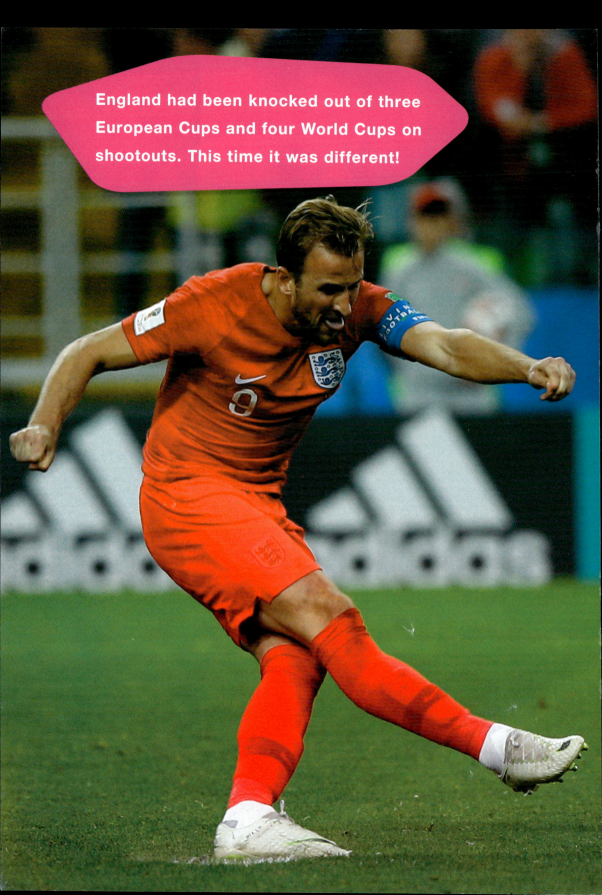

In 2018, England reached the World Cup **knockout stage**. Now the team faced a penalty shootout against Colombia. If they won, England would reach their first quarter-final in 12 years. But England had often lost penalty shootouts. Would history repeat itself? The pressure was huge.

Harry Kane stepped forward to take his penalty. He drilled the ball into the left corner. The crowd roared. Harry had done his bit. The shootout was over. England had won 4–3!

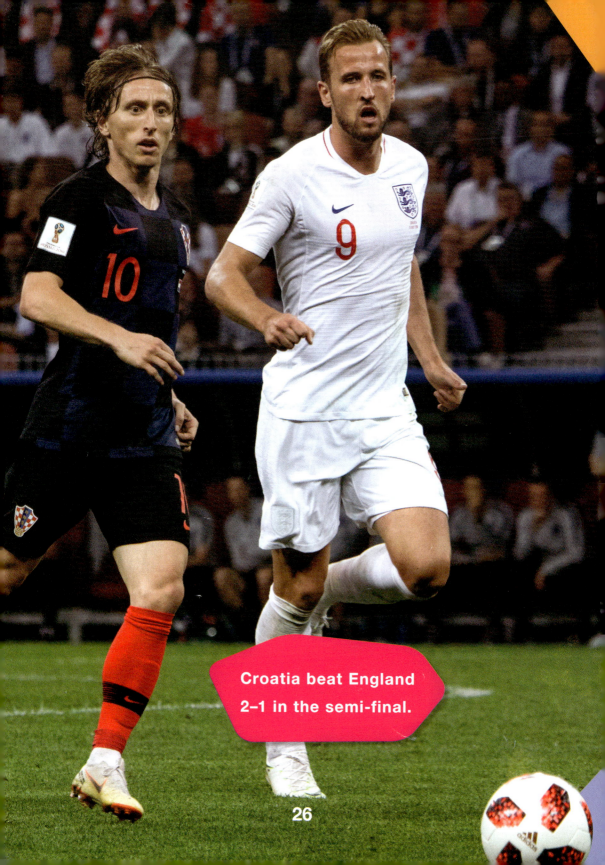

Croatia beat England 2–1 in the semi-final.

After the Colombia match, England was buzzing. Some thought the team could win the World Cup. But it wasn't to be. England were knocked out in the semi-finals. However, the World Cup had been a triumph for Harry. He won the Golden Boot award for the most World Cup goals scored.

Harry was once the small street player from North London. But now, he had won the success, fame and fortune he had always dreamed of.

GLOSSARY

academy
part of a football club that signs players at a young age

determined
making a firm decision about something and sticking to it

hat trick
when one player scores three goals in a match

knockout stage
the point in a tournament when a team is eliminated if they lose a match

loan
sent out to join another club for a temporary period

injury time
time added to the end of a match because of injuries during normal play

penalty shootout
deciding a match through penalties when there is no winning team after normal play

scout
someone who looks for talented footballers to sign to a club

striker
forward player who is expected to score goals

youth club
football club for child players who are still at school

TIMELINE

1993: Harry Edward Kane is born in Walthamstow, London, England.

1999–2001: Harry plays for Ridgeway Rovers.

2001–2002: Harry joins Arsenal's youth academy.

2004: Harry joins Tottenham Hotspur's youth academy.

2010–2015: Harry plays for the England Under-17, Under-19, Under-20 and Under-21 teams.

2011–2013: Harry is loaned out to Leyton Orient, Millwall, Norwich City and Leicester City.

2015: Harry becomes Tottenham's highest scorer in one season.

2015: Harry makes his first appearance for the England senior team.

2018: Harry wins the Golden Boot award at the 2018 World Cup in Russia.

ACTIVITY

WRITE A BIOGRAPHY OF YOUR FAVOURITE FOOTBALLER

Who is your favourite footballer? What were their lives like before they became famous? Did they suffer early disappointments like Harry Kane did? Why not write a short biography on them? It's a great way to learn about a hero. There is plenty of information on the internet about players. Remember to keep your biography short. Only include the interesting and important bits. You could show it to your teacher, friends and family afterwards. One day, maybe you could write about football for a job!

FIND OUT MORE

Love reading about football? Learn more here:

Books

Football (Fantastic Sport Facts), Michael Hurley (Raintree, 2014)

Spotlight on the World Cup (Young Explorer), Chris Oxlade (Raintree 2017)

Top Football Tips (Snap Books: Top Sports Tips), Danielle S. Hammelef (Raintree, 2018)

Websites

The English Football Association website where you can find out about footballers in the England team:
www.thefa.com

The English Premier League website which provides information about games and players:
www.premierleague.com

INDEX